Copyright © 2026 Claire Melanie Barnett
All rights reserved.

No part of this publication may be reproduced, distributed, stored in a retrieval system, or transmitted in any form or by any means — electronic, mechanical, photocopying, recording, or otherwise — without prior written permission from the copyright holder, except in the case of brief quotations used in reviews or other
non-commercial uses permitted under applicable copyright law.

ISBN: 978-1-7646510-0-4
Published by Wild Truth Press
First Edition — 2026

This publication is distributed internationally.
Manufacturing location may vary.

AF889198

DISCLAIMER

This journal is an educational and reflective resource intended to support personal awareness and self-understanding following experiences of abuse.

It is informed by lived experience and widely recognised trauma-informed principles regarding the psychological, emotional, neurological, and relational impact of abuse.

The author is not acting in the capacity of a licensed therapist, psychologist, medical practitioner, legal adviser, or crisis service provider.

This journal does not provide therapy, diagnosis, treatment, legal advice, or crisis intervention.

It is not a substitute for professional mental health care, medical care, legal consultation, or emergency services.

Abuse, coercive control, and domestic violence involve complex psychological and safety considerations.

Situations may escalate unpredictably.

Readers remain solely responsible for their own decisions, safety planning, and actions.

If you are in immediate danger, contact emergency services in your area.

If you require specialised support, seek assistance from a qualified professional, domestic violence service, crisis line, legal adviser, or medical provider.

The examples, scenarios, and narratives contained within this journal are illustrative in nature and are designed to demonstrate common behavioural patterns reported by survivors.

They do not represent any specific individual and are not intended to diagnose, label, or legally define any person or situation.

While every effort has been made to present information responsibly and accurately, no guarantees are made regarding outcomes.

The author and publisher disclaim liability for any direct, indirect, incidental, or consequential loss, injury, damage, or harm arising from the use of this journal.

Use of this journal constitutes acceptance of these terms.

Dedication

This is dedicated to every woman who has lived inside abuse — the ones still in it, the ones walking out of it, and the ones slowly finding their way back to themselves.

Not everyone will understand what you've carried. But the women who have lived it are your sisters. We see you. We recognise the confusion, the strength it took to survive, and the quiet clarity that eventually begins to rise after it.

May this journal help you see more clearly, trust yourself sooner, and understand that what happened to you was never a reflection of your worth.

May your future feel safer, lighter, and truly your own. And may your abuse, your abuser, and even this journal one day sit firmly in your past — as part of your story, but not your present — while you live a life that is full of love, calm, and free.

WHAT THIS JOURNAL WILL HELP YOU DO

This journal is designed to help you make sense of what happened to you — in a way that feels clear, grounding, and honest.

Inside, you will:

- Understand what actually happened — without minimising it or questioning yourself
- Recognise patterns of confusion, control, and abuse more clearly
- Separate what is real from what you were made to believe
- Make sense of your thoughts, feelings, and reactions
- Feel less overwhelmed and more steady in yourself
- Rebuild trust in your instincts and your perception
- Understand the impact of the relationship — without self-blame
- Begin reconnecting with who you are, outside of what you've been through
- Move from confusion toward clarity — one step at a time

This is not about rushing your healing.
It is about helping you see clearly,
so you can begin to move forward in a way that feels right for you.

TABLE OF CONTENTS

BEFORE YOU BEGIN

If you feel confused — this is for you.
If you keep questioning yourself — this is for you.
If you're trying to make sense of something that doesn't add up — this is for you.
If you've found yourself going over the same moments, trying to understand what really happened — this is for you.
If part of you knows something wasn't right, but you can't fully explain why — this is for you.
You don't need to have the right words yet.
You don't need to have clarity yet.
You just need a place to start.
This journal is here to help you untangle what feels confusing,
to make sense of what you've experienced,
and to slowly bring you back to yourself — at your own pace.

SAFETY & SUPPORT

IF YOU NEED IMMEDIATE SUPPORT

If you are in immediate danger, contact your local emergency services immediately.

If you are not in immediate danger but you feel unsafe, overwhelmed, or unsure what to do next, please reach out to a trusted person or a local support service in your country.

Many countries have organisations that provide confidential support for people experiencing domestic abuse, family violence, coercive control, sexual violence, or mental health crises. If you are unsure where to begin, your local healthcare provider, crisis service, hospital, or emergency services can help connect you with the right support.

You do not have to be physically injured to deserve help.

If something feels wrong...
If you feel frightened...
If you feel like you're constantly questioning yourself...
Your experience matters.

If using your phone or computer could place you at greater risk, wait until it is safe to seek help, or use a device your abusive partner cannot access if possible.

You deserve to feel safe.
You deserve to be believed.
You do not have to navigate this alone.

YOUR SAFETY COMES FIRST

If you are currently living with someone who is abusive or controlling, your safety is always more important than finishing this journal.

Leaving an abusive relationship is not always simple.

It often requires planning, support, and careful timing.

If leaving may increase your risk, consider making plans quietly rather than confronting the person about what you have discovered.

You do not owe anyone an explanation before protecting yourself.

If it is safe to do so, you may wish to begin preparing things gradually.

- Save important documents somewhere safe.
- Keep emergency contacts somewhere you can access them.
- Think about a trusted person you could contact if you needed help.
- Consider where you could go if you needed to leave quickly.
- If possible, keep a small bag of essentials somewhere safe.

Every situation is different.
Only you know what feels safest for you.
This journal is not asking you to leave today.
It is asking you to understand what has been happening to you.
Understanding brings clarity.
Clarity helps you make safer decisions when the time is right.

Your safety will always come first.

UNDERSTANDING COERCIVE CONTROL

If you've picked up this journal, there's a good chance you're trying to understand what happened to you. You may have experienced emotional abuse, psychological abuse, verbal abuse, financial abuse, sexual abuse, physical abuse—or perhaps a combination of many different behaviours. While these forms of abuse can look very different from one relationship to another, many are connected by one underlying pattern: coercive control.

Coercive control is not a single event or one obvious act of abuse. It is an ongoing pattern of behaviours used to influence, manipulate, intimidate, isolate, or control another person. It often develops so gradually that it can be difficult to recognise while you're living through it. Instead of noticing the pattern, you simply find yourself adapting to it.

Many people think abuse begins with physical violence, but for many survivors it begins with confusion. The control may come through constant criticism, intimidation, guilt, monitoring your movements, controlling money, isolating you from people you love, making you question your own memory, or giving affection one moment only to withdraw it the next. Although the behaviours themselves may differ, they often serve the same purpose: slowly shifting the balance of power until you begin questioning yourself instead of questioning what is happening to you.

Over time, these experiences can change far more than the relationship itself. They can affect how safe you feel, how much you trust your own instincts, how you see yourself, and even how your nervous system responds to everyday life. You may find yourself explaining less, apologising more, avoiding certain conversations, walking on eggshells, or constantly trying to predict someone else's reactions. Little by little, your world becomes smaller, not because you chose it, but because adapting felt like the safest way to survive.

This is why understanding coercive control is so important. It helps explain why abuse is often so difficult to recognise while you're living through it, why leaving isn't always simple, and why your body and mind may still be responding long after the relationship has changed. Most importantly, it helps you understand that your reactions were not signs of weakness. They were human responses to repeated manipulation, fear, and control.

This journal is not here to diagnose your relationship or tell you what decisions to make. It is here to help you recognise patterns, make sense of your experiences, and begin rebuilding trust in yourself. Because recognition comes before healing, and understanding what happened is often the first step towards finding yourself again.

WHAT THIS JOURNAL IS — AND HOW TO USE IT

This journal is written in stages because when you've lived through abuse, everything feels tangled and upside down.

I wrote it this way to help you untangle it slowly — to understand what happened, to quiet the self-blame, and to find your footing again.

It's best followed in order, but there is no rush. You can pause, come back, and move at your own pace.
This was created by someone who has lived it and understands how confusing it can feel.

You are not alone here, and you don't have to figure it all out at once.

HOW TO MOVE THROUGH THIS JOURNAL

This journal is structured in stages for a reason.

Each stage supports a different phase of clarity, safety, and rebuilding after a harmful or abusive dynamic.

Some women will move through it quickly.
Some will pause.
Some will return to earlier sections more than once.

Your timing matters.

If you are still in active contact, still feeling pulled back in, still trying to understand what happened, or still negotiating safety, earlier stages may be more appropriate.

If you are physically safe and emotionally distancing yourself, later stages may land more deeply.

You may move forward.
You may circle back.
You may repeat a stage more than once.

That is not regression.
It is reinforcement.

There is no correct speed.
Only alignment.

STAGE ONE
ORIENTATION

This stage is about understanding what has happened and grounding yourself in where you are now.

You are not here to fix anything.
You are not here to make decisions or take action.

You are here to make sense of your experience and steady yourself.

Nothing needs to be resolved.
Nothing needs to be uncovered or explained.

Awareness comes before change.
Clarity comes before direction.

For now, your only task is to notice, to name, and to be honest with yourself — at your own pace.

You have been through something that affected your body, your mind, and your sense of safety.
What you lived through matters because of the impact it had on you — not because of how it looks from the outside.

You are not expected to be okay here.
You are allowed to take your time.

WHAT LED YOU TO THIS MOMENT

You might write about what made you reach for this book, what you're carrying right now, or what you're hoping might feel different one day. There is no right way to fill this page.

WHAT I NEED RIGHT NOW

You might write about what feels hardest to live with right now, what you're tired of carrying, or what you wish could feel different.

This isn't about fixing everything.

It's about noticing what matters most in this moment.

WHERE ARE YOU RIGHT NOW?

Where are you right now in the relationship?

- ☐ I have left
- ☐ I am still there
- ☐ I am in between
- ☐ I'm thinking about it
- ☐ I'm planning quietly
- ☐ I'm just trying to get through each day

If you are still there or in between, what best describes where you're at with the idea of leaving?

____

____

____

It is very common to leave while still hoping things might change — or to stay while quietly planning. Both are survival responses.

YOUR CURRENT SITUATION

Do you feel physically safe right now?

Do you have a place you could go if things escalated?

What support do you have right now?

Who knows what is really happening?

What do you not have yet that you may need?

CONFUSION FROM INCONSISTENCY IS NOT WEAKNESS

It is very common to feel torn — even to leave while still hoping things might change. You are navigating fear, attachment, and safety at the same time, and that is overwhelming.

Feeling foggy, exhausted, or emotionally up and down is your nervous system responding exactly as it was designed to after prolonged stress. This is your body trying to protect you.

Sometimes you may feel weak for wishing things were different, or for still wanting someone who hurt you.

There is nothing wrong with you. Feeling this way is completely normal when someone has shown you both love and harm. When a person can be kind one day and cruel the next, it creates confusion.

Your reactions are a human response to inconsistency — not a reflection of weakness.

BELIEFS CAN KEEP YOU STUCK

Sometimes we don't stay because we want to. We stay because everything is tangled. Beliefs, family, expectation, our fears, our hopes, and the opinions of others. It can be from what we were taught growing up, or a version of our abuser we are still holding onto.

Tick anything that feels familiar, past or present.

- ☐ If I can just avoid upsetting him, things will stay calm.
- ☐ If I leave, it will be worse — for me or for the children.
- ☐ He can be a good father, even if he isn't good to me.
- ☐ Other people say it's not that bad — at least he doesn't hit me.
- ☐ Maybe I'm overreacting.
- ☐ I'm just trying to get through each day
- ☐ Maybe this is partly my fault.
- ☐ If I try harder, the kind version of him will come back.
- ☐ I don't want to break up my family.
- ☐ This is just how relationships are.
- ☐ This is how men are.
- ☐ I've seen worse.

UNDERSTANDING THESE BELIEFS

These thoughts are shaped by experience — sometimes long before this relationship began, and sometimes reinforced inside it. Becoming aware of them is not about blaming yourself. It is how we begin to move away from them.

Write a belief that never truly felt like yours — something you carried because it was repeated, expected, or imposed, but deep down never fit.

The stories in this journal are illustrative examples created for educational and reflective purposes to help identify behavioural patterns and deepen understanding.

WHY DID THIS HAPPEN TO ME?

One of the most confusing parts of a relationship like this is how quickly a normal moment can turn. It often starts with something ordinary.

You might say, "I'm going to give my friend a call."

And suddenly it's not ordinary anymore.

"Your friend?" "What do you mean your friend?" "You were saying yesterday how annoying she is."

You pause. Because yes — yesterday she annoyed you. She cut you off mid-sentence. You were venting. It meant nothing.

Before you can explain that, it keeps going.

"Oh, so you're that type of person, are you?" "Talk shit about your friends one day and call them the next." "That's fucked."

Now you're confused. Are you defending yourself, or explaining something that shouldn't need explaining? You try to speak. "I didn't mean—" But it's already moved.

"She's a fuckhead anyway." "I don't even know why you're friends with her."

Now you're not defending yourself anymore. Now you're defending your friend. Your brain scrambles. I said she annoyed me. That doesn't mean I hate her. Everyone knows that.

You open your mouth to say it.

Not just on your thoughts — but on your sense of who you are. They can make you question your values. Your intentions. Your morality. They can leave you wondering whether you were kind or cruel. Loyal or dishonest. A good person or a bad one.

The confusion you are experiencing is recognised in psychology. Feeling disoriented, self-doubting, and unsure of what just happened is a common response when someone is exposed to psychologically abusive behaviour — particularly emotional and coercive control.

Interactions like the one described above are often how this kind of abuse begins and escalates over time.

When a person is repeatedly exposed to these dynamics, their nervous system shifts into survival mode. In that state, the brain prioritises safety over clarity.

That's why your thoughts scatter. That's why you freeze. That's why you can't organise words the way you normally would.

This confusion is not a failure. It is a physiological response to threat. Healthy relationships do not require you to explain normal human behaviour. Feeling annoyed with a friend, venting, changing your mind, loving someone even when they frustrate you — these things do not need defending in safe relationships.

In these relationships it is normal to feel love, attachment, or loyalty — and still be harmed. Those feelings do not mean what happened was okay.

These people do not behave randomly. These interactions follow patterns. The patterns repeat. And they are often strategic — not in a dramatic or cinematic way, but in a way that is practiced, familiar, and effective.

For the person using these behaviours, the interactions don't feel complicated. They feel easy.

That ease is what makes you doubt yourself. But ease doesn't mean truth.

"If you let her come over, I'll tell her everything you've said about her."
"She deserves to know what kind of person you are."

Your stomach drops. Now there's fear. You're trying to catch up to the conversation, but it's moving too fast. You don't even know what the argument is about anymore.

Then another turn.

"I've seen the way she looks at you." "She judges you." "I bet she thinks you're fat."

Minutes ago, you were making a phone call. Now you're questioning your friend, yourself, your body, your intentions. Do I actually hate my friend? Does she hate me? Am I a bad friend? Did I do something wrong?

Every word being used against you came from something you once said in trust. And it all happened so fast that you feel overwhelmed and very confused. You think: Why is this so easy for them? Why can't I explain myself properly? Maybe it really is me.

This is the moment that changes everything.
Because what you experienced there wasn't a misunderstanding. It wasn't a communication issue. And it wasn't because you're bad with words.

You were or are in a relationship with someone who moves strategically and designs interactions to control and confuse.

When these behaviours are used on you, they have effects.
And it never meant you were the problem.

Understanding what is happening in your relationship is powerful. It doesn't mean you have to act. It doesn't mean you have to decide anything yet. It simply means you are no longer in the dark.

What you have been through is traumatic. This journal is designed for you to move at your own pace.
You don't need to hold all of this at once. You can put it down and take a break whenever you need.

You weren't weak. You weren't naïve.
You were human — responding emotionally and in real time — in a relationship where the other person's abusive behaviour was structured to work, to control, to scare, to frighten, harm, and to not be fair.

These examples describe common patterns reported by many survivors.

Not every experience looks the same.

NERVOUS SYSTEM CHECK-IN

This is a simple, proven way to bring your body out of stress and back into the present moment.

Pause here.

Take a breath.

Look around you.

Name 3 things you can see.

2 things you can feel.

1 thing you can hear.

You are here.
Right now.
Nothing else needs to be figured out in this moment.

WHAT I FEARED WOULD HAPPEN IF I LEFT

Tick anything that feels familiar — past or present

- ☐ If I leave, things could become worse.
- ☐ I might regret it.
- ☐ I might not cope on my own.
- ☐ I could lose stability.
- ☐ Other people might judge me.
- ☐ I might break something that can't be repaired.
- ☐ Maybe it isn't "bad enough" to leave.
- ☐ Maybe I am overreacting.
- ☐ Maybe this is just how relationships are.

PAUSE HERE

You have the right to feel safe in your own home.

You have the right to live without fear,
intimidation, or constantly being on edge.

If you are a mother, your children deserve safety and steadiness too.
If you are not, you still deserve those things
fully and completely.

No form of abuse — loud or quiet,
obvious or subtle — is something you
are required to endure.

Leaving is not a grand statement.

Sometimes it is simply a quiet moment of clarity.
It isn't about having everything figured out.
It can be a decision made in worry,
fear, and sometimes chaos.
It can be choosing a little more calm.
A little more steadiness.
A little more safety.
It can be remembering what it feels like
to have a settled nervous system — and listening
to what you need in that moment.

ABUSE AWARENESS CHECKLIST

These pages exist to help you name what you've lived through — especially the things that are often minimised, normalised, or misunderstood.

You do not need to tick everything.
You do not need to explain or justify any of this.

(Tick anything that feels familiar — past or present)

PHYSICAL ABUSE

□ Any form of physical harm
□ Restraint or blocking your movement
□ Physical intimidation
□ Being grabbed, pushed, hit, or hurt
□ Fear of physical escalation

DIGITAL / TECHNOLOGICAL ABUSE

□ Monitoring your phone, messages, or social media
□ Demanding passwords or access
□ Tracking your location
□ Using technology to intimidate or control
□ Harassment through messages or online platforms

EMOTIONAL & PSYCHOLOGICAL ABUSE

□ Being made to feel "too sensitive," dramatic, or irrational

□ Being blamed for the other person's reactions or behaviour

□ Constant criticism, belittling, or humiliation

□ Being mocked, ridiculed, or spoken to with contempt

□ Having your feelings dismissed, ignored, or twisted

□ Being made to doubt your memory, perception, or sanity

□ Feeling confused after conversations

□ Apologies that turned into blame

□ Being punished emotionally (silence, withdrawal, coldness)

□ Feeling like you had to walk on eggshells

COERCIVE CONTROL

□ Feeling monitored, watched, or controlled

□ Being told what you could wear, say, post, or think

□ Rules that applied to you but not to them

□ Fear of consequences if you disagreed or said no

□ Having to ask permission for normal things

□ Feeling like your autonomy slowly disappeared

□ Being made dependent over time

□ Feeling trapped without knowing exactly why

GASLIGHTING

□ Being told events didn't happen the way you remember

□ Being told you were imagining things

□ Having facts denied or rewritten

□ Being accused of lying when you were telling the truth

□ Feeling mentally foggy or disoriented

□ Second-guessing yourself constantly

□ Feeling like you couldn't trust your own mind

VERBAL ABUSE

□ Being shouted at, sworn at, or spoken to aggressively

□ Threatening language or tone

□ Name-calling or insults

□ Sarcasm meant to hurt or control

□ Statements meant to intimidate or silence you

□ Being spoken to as if you were inferior

INTIMIDATION & THREATS

□ Threats of harm (to you, themselves, others, pets, or property)

□ Threats of abandonment or punishment

□ Slamming doors, breaking things, or violent gestures

□ Using anger or rage to control outcomes

□ Feeling afraid of how they might react

FINANCIAL ABUSE

□ Being controlled through money

□ Not being allowed access to finances

□ Being kept financially dependent

□ Having spending monitored or criticised

□ Being sabotaged financially

□ Being left with debt or financial stress

□ Being prevented from working or studying

SOCIAL ISOLATION

□ Being discouraged from seeing friends or family

□ Being made to feel guilty for outside connections

□ Having relationships undermined

□ Being made to choose between them and others

□ Feeling alone even when not physically isolated

SEXUAL COERCION OR VIOLATION

□ Pressure to engage in sexual activity

□ Feeling obligated rather than consenting

□ Being guilted, manipulated, or punished sexually

□ Sexual boundaries being ignored

□ Feeling unsafe or disconnected during intimacy

□ Sex being used as control or leverage

THIS PAGE IS FOR WHATEVER IS SITTING WITH YOU NOW — EMOTIONALLY, MENTALLY, OR PHYSICALLY — AFTER NAMING YOUR EXPERIENCE AND SEEING IT MORE CLEARLY.

This is simply a place to let your body and mind respond.
There is no right response. Nothing needs to make sense.

AFTER EFFECTS OF ABUSE
COMMON TRAUMA RESPONSES

(Tick anything that feels familiar)

☐ Hypervigilance

☐ Anxiety or panic

☐ Emotional numbness

☐ Difficulty trusting yourself

☐ Difficulty trusting others

☐ Shame or self-blame

☐ Confusion about what was "real"

☐ Feeling disconnected from who you were before

Abuse does not need to look a certain way to be real.
What matters is how it affected you.
This checklist is here to help you understand what you're healing from.

What stands out to you on this page?
Write anything you want to notice, question, or say to yourself.

LET IT KEEP COMING

This page is here if there's more that wants to come out.

You don't need to make sense of it.
You don't need to finish a thought.
You don't need to stay with one feeling.

CHECK-IN (USE ANYTIME)

You don't need to tick them all.
You don't need to feel ready.
Some days you feel clear.
Other days you feel confused again.
Confusion is real.
It runs deep.
It affects your body, your thoughts, and your confidence. Clarity doesn't have to be loud.
Sometimes it is quiet.
Sometimes it is just a small knowing in your chest.
And that is enough.

Tick what feels true — today, not forever.

□ I feel safer than I did before.

□ I trust myself more than I used to.

□ I understand my feelings better.

□ I'm less hard on myself.

□ I'm learning what I need.

□ I'm moving forward — even slowly.

□ I can see change, even if it's small.

□ I feel less confused than I did before.

□ I have moments of clarity about what I want — even if I'm still scared.

□ I can imagine a future that feels calmer, safer, or more mine.

WHAT FEELS EVEN A LITTLE BIT BETTER THAN IT USED TO?

COME BACK TO YOUR BODY

Small physical shifts like relaxing your shoulders and unclenching your jaw signal safety to your nervous system.

Just pause for a second.

Drop your shoulders.

Unclench your jaw.

Take a slow breath in... and out.

You don't have to hold
everything at once.

You're allowed to take this
one page at a time.

Come back to this whenever you need.

STAGE TWO
CLARITY

This stage is about understanding how this experience has affected you — emotionally, psychologically, and physically — and how it shaped the way you feel, think, and respond.

What you are feeling may still feel close or overwhelming, even if the situation has changed. That does not mean you are stuck. It means what happened to you had a real impact.

Someone caused this harm. Someone crossed lines, manipulated, controlled, and hurt you. What happened was not accidental — and it was not because of who you are.

This stage is not about excusing what happened. It is about understanding it clearly enough that you no longer carry responsibility for it.

As patterns become clearer, self-blame often begins to loosen and shame starts to lift.

What you experienced may have altered how safe you feel, how you see yourself, and what you believe you deserve.

WHAT YOU'RE FEELING IS REAL — AND IT MATTERS

This journal honours the depth of your hurt — the betrayal, the grief, and the shock of realising that someone you trusted was capable of causing you this pain.

You are allowed to be devastated.
You are allowed to be confused and clear at the same time.
You are allowed to learn, to feel, and to begin seeing yourself more kindly as the fog slowly starts to lift.

THIS IS WHERE THE IMPACT LANDS

Write about the impact this experience has had on you.
Your self-worth. Your confidence. How you feel in social situations or relationships. What feels different about you now.
A page to notice the impact of what happened to you.

WHAT FEELS HEAVY RIGHT NOW

Just name it. No fixing. No explaining.

HOW HAS THIS AFFECTED YOUR INNER WORLD (THE IMPACT OF THIS RELATIONSHIP)

The behaviours you were exposed to don't just hurt you — they affect how you see yourself, how safe you feel, and how much you trust yourself.

Did this relationship change the way you see yourself?

☐ Yes ☐ No

Did this relationship affect how safe you feel in your own body or mind?

☐ Yes ☐ No

Did this relationship impact how much you trust your instincts or judgement?

☐ Yes ☐ No

SUSTAINED HARM

Sustained harm alters your sense of safety,
your self-trust, and the way you move through the world.

If you feel on edge, hyper-aware, or constantly bracing,
that is not a weakness.
It is what your body learned to do to keep you safe.

What you have lived through does not just stay in the past.

Nothing about what you are feeling is an overreaction.

Nothing about this is "too much."

Your body adapted to survive something that felt unsafe,
unpredictable, or overwhelming.
And you are allowed to take the time you need
to feel safe again.

You can pause here.

You don't need to take this any further right now.

HOW HAS THIS AFFECTED YOUR OUTER WORLD

(the impact of this relationship)

What you lived through may have changed how you relate to others and how you move through the world.

Did this relationship affect how you show up in relationships now?
☐ Yes ☐ No

Did this relationship affect your boundaries or ability to say no?
☐ Yes ☐ No

Did this relationship lead to hypervigilance, people pleasing, or withdrawing?
☐ Yes ☐ No

This stage is about gently understanding how this experience has affected you.
Not just what happened — but what it did to your sense of safety, trust, identity, and self-worth.
When an offender repeatedly harms, manipulates, or controls you, the impact does not end when the abuse ends. It can change how you see yourself, how safe the world feels, how your body reacts, and what you believe you deserve.
These effects can show up in different ways, and to different degrees, across all forms of abuse — emotional, psychological, financial, physical, sexual, or controlling.

This journal sees you.
It understands how hard you were trying to survive what was done to you.

Your response to this abuse — and the way you feel now — comes from your system trying to protect you.
Nothing about this is wrong.
Many of the decisions you made were not choices — they were survival responses.

BEFORE THE OFFENDER ENTERED YOUR LIFE

Before the offender entered your life, you were not weak, naïve, or broken.

You may have been shy.
You may have been empathetic.
You may have been open-hearted, emotionally available, trusting, generous.

Some people enter abusive relationships repeating familiar patterns from earlier life.
Others enter believing the world is mostly safe,
that love is mutual,
and that harm is obvious when it appears.

Across different experiences, one thing is often true:

Before the offender, you were lighter.

You trusted more easily.
You believed love was real and protective.
You did not live on constant alert.

What changed most was not your personality.

It was your sense of safety, trust, and worth.

Those are not things you chose to lose.
They are things that were taken.

HOW THE OFFENDER DESTABILISES

Abusive offenders do not usually begin with cruelty.
They begin with connection.

They may idolise you.
Make you feel chosen.
Wrap control in affection, pride, or belonging.

Possessiveness can be introduced in ways that feel flattering, not threatening.
Jealousy can be framed as care.
Intensity can be framed as love.

Then the pattern begins.

Affection may be withdrawn without explanation.
Emotional, sexual, verbal, or financial rejection can appear suddenly.
When you ask what's wrong, the offender may deny there is a problem.

You are left alone with unanswered questions.

So your mind fills the gaps.

What did I do wrong?
Why am I suddenly not enough?
Maybe I'm taking this too personally.

That is not insecurity.

That is conditioning.

ESCALATION AND PSYCHOLOGICAL ENTRAPMENT

Over time, the offender escalates.

Love followed by cruelty.
Cruelty followed by apology.
Apology followed by hope.

Verbal, emotional, physical, sexual, or financial harm reinforces fears planted earlier.
Past trauma stories may be used to excuse present abuse.
Just enough remorse may be shown to keep you attached.

When you try to pull away, the offender may re-enter.

This creates confusion.
Hope mixed with fear.
A growing need for relief from pain they are causing.

Eventually, many people begin to believe what the offender says about them.

That no one else would want them.
That staying is safer than leaving.
That they are responsible for fixing something.

This is not a relationship problem.

This is psychological entrapment by an offender.

ROLES, RULES, AND SURVIVAL

The offender does not only abuse you.
They force you into a role.

The role may look different for different people,
but it often involves managing the offender's moods, needs, or reactions.

Alongside the role come rules — often unspoken.

Who you talk to.
What you say.
How you behave.
What feels "safe" to ask for.
How to avoid setting them off.

Life becomes organised around managing harm.
You were not staying because you wanted to.
You were managing danger.

Explaining does not stop abuse.
Loving harder does not stop abuse.
Complying does not stop abuse.

What often develops instead is adaptation.

Staying alert.
Staying quiet.
Staying alive.

This is not weakness.
It is survival under threat.

NERVOUS SYSTEM CHECK-IN

This is a simple, proven way to bring your body out of stress and back into the present moment.

Pause here.

Take a breath.

Look around you.

Name 3 things you can see.

2 things you can feel.

1 thing you can hear.

You are here.
Right now.
Nothing else needs to be figured out in this moment.

AFTER THE ABUSE

People who have not lived this
often misunderstand one thing.

They think:
If someone hurts you, you leave.

What they do not understand is this:

Abusive offenders are often intentional, strategic, and unpredictable.
That combination is frightening.

You were not responding to one incident.
You were navigating a psychological minefield.

Leaving in this environment is not a simple decision.
It is an escape window.
And when that window appears,
many people take it.

Even long after abuse ends,
the body may still respond as if danger is possible.
This can include sudden adrenaline,
hyper-alertness,
freezing or fighting responses,
or difficulty trusting others.

These reactions are not choices.
They exist because someone interfered with your sense of safety and reality.
Your body is not betraying you. It is remembering.

WHAT LIVING THROUGH ABUSE DID TO ME

What it took. What it changed.

Below are common effects of abuse reported by many survivors. These can occur across all forms of abuse — emotional, psychological, financial, physical, sexual, or controlling — and may show up in different ways or to different degrees.

Tick anything that feels true for you. Leave anything that doesn't. There is no right or wrong response.

□ My sense of safety has changed
□ I feel more on edge, alert, or guarded than I used to
□ I struggle to relax, even when nothing is "wrong"

□ My self-worth has been affected
□ I doubt myself more than I used to
□ I feel "less than," ashamed, or not good enough

□ I question my judgment or instincts
□ I second-guess my decisions
□ I worry about getting things wrong

□ My body reacts strongly to stress or conflict
□ I experience sudden anxiety, adrenaline, or panic
□ I freeze, shut down, fight back, or feel overwhelmed
□ I feel disconnected from parts of myself

□ I don't recognise who I am anymore

□ I miss who I used to be

□ My trust in others has changed

□ I find it hard to trust people's intentions

□ I feel safer keeping distance from others

□ My relationships feel harder to navigate

□ I people-please, withdraw, or stay quiet to avoid conflict

□ I feel responsible for keeping things calm

□ I feel emotionally numb or detached at times

□ I swing between intense emotion and feeling nothing

□ I struggle to name what I feel

□ My confidence in social situations has changed

□ I feel watched, judged, or out of place

□ I avoid situations I once felt comfortable in

□ I carry fear, even though the abuse has ended

□ I feel like danger could return at any time

□ I stay prepared for things to go wrong

□ I feel grief for what this took from me

□ I mourn the version of myself I was before

□ I feel sadness about what could have been

☐ I feel anger — at the offender, the situation, or myself

☐ I feel shame or self-blame

☐ I wonder why this happened to me

TAKE A MOMENT HERE.

Naming these changes is not you falling apart — it is you making sense of what was done to you.

Placing this on the page helps your system organise what happened, instead of carrying it as confusion or self-blame. Bringing this into awareness is not meant to hurt you — it's meant to steady you. Clarity calms the nervous system.

What you've marked here means you adapted to survive an offender who caused real harm.

After seeing this clearly, what do you want back more than anything?

HOW THIS EXPERIENCE AFFECTED YOU

This page is here not for what was done to you,
but how what was done to you changed you.
This is simply a place to let your system respond.
There is no right response. Nothing needs to make sense.

LET IT KEEP COMING (IF YOU NEED)

This page is here if there's more that wants to come out.
You don't need to make sense of it.
You don't need to finish a thought.
You don't need to stay with one feeling.

NOTICING WHAT HAPPENS

Abuse doesn't usually happen once. It happens in patterns. One of the most important patterns is what happens when you respond — and what happens when you don't.

This is to help you become aware of the pattern, so it no longer feels random, unpredictable, or overwhelming.

What I've noticed when I respond to the abuse:

What I've noticed when I don't respond to the abuse:

What behaviour from them shows up no matter what I do?

How I feel when I respond / how I feel when I don't respond:

CHECK-IN (USE ANYTIME)

You don't need to tick them all.
You don't need to feel ready.
Some days clarity comes first.
Other days it fades.
This page is here to remind you that confusion is not failure and clarity doesn't have to be loud to be real.

Tick what feels true — today, not forever.

□ I feel safer than I did before.

□ I trust myself more than I used to.

□ I understand my feelings better.

□ I'm less hard on myself.

□ I'm learning what I need.

□ I'm moving forward — even slowly.

□ I can see change, even if it's small.

□ I feel less confused than I did before.

□ I have moments of clarity about what I want — even if I'm still scared.

□ I can imagine a future that feels calmer, safer, or more mine.

YOU CAN STOP HERE

You can stop here if you need to.

You don't have to keep going just because you started.

Close the book.

Come back later.

Or don't.

There is no rush.

You do this in your own time.

STAGE THREE
STABILISATION

This stage is about helping your body and nervous system settle after living in prolonged stress, fear, or unpredictability.

Even when danger has passed, your body may still respond as if it hasn't. This does not mean you are broken. It means your system learned how to survive.

You are not here to push through.
You are not here to process everything at once.
You are not here to "be strong."

You are here to slow down, ground, and gently reconnect with a sense of safety inside yourself.

Nothing needs to be fixed.
Nothing needs to be forced.

Stabilisation comes before rebuilding.
Safety comes before growth.

You are allowed to move slowly here.

STABILISATION IS NOT ABOUT FEELING CALM ALL THE TIME

It is about having moments where your body feels
a little less on edge.

A little less braced.

A little less alert.

You may still feel anxious, tired, foggy, or emotional.
That is normal at this stage.

Your nervous system spent a long time responding to threat.

It does not switch off on command.

This stage is about helping your system learn that
right now — in this moment —
you are not under attack.

Even brief moments of grounding matter.

Nothing you feel here is wrong.

WHEN PEOPLE ASK QUESTIONS THAT HURT

People who haven't lived through abuse often ask questions that feel confronting or painful — especially while you're still in it, or after you've left.

Questions like:
Why didn't you just leave?
Why did you stay so long?
If it was that bad, why did you go back?

These questions usually come from not understanding how abuse actually works.

You don't have to explain yourself.
But if you choose to respond, here are two options.

If you don't want to explain:
I'm focusing on healing right now.
I don't feel able to explain my experience.

If you choose to educate:
Leaving wasn't a simple choice — it required planning an escape.
Staying was about staying safe. Leaving is often the most dangerous time.

People do need to be educated about the impact of abuse.
Your silence is also allowed.

You choose.

HOW MY BODY FEELS RIGHT NOW

Notice what is happening in your body — without trying to change it. You might write about tension, fatigue, restlessness, numbness, heaviness, alertness,
discomfort, or anything else you notice.

There is no correct way to describe this.
You are simply noticing.

WHEN I FEEL MOST UNSETTLED

You might write about moments when your body feels most activated.
Times of day. Certain conversations. Specific places. Silence. Conflict. Being alone. Being around others.

This is not about avoiding life.
It is about understanding your system so it feels less confusing and overwhelming.

WHEN I FEEL EVEN A LITTLE SAFER

Write about moments — even small ones — when your body feels slightly more settled.
This could be a place, a person, a routine, a time of day, a sensory experience, being distracted, being still.

You are not required to feel "safe" all the time.
We are only noticing what helps — even a little.

COME BACK TO YOUR BODY

Small physical shifts like relaxing your shoulders and unclenching your jaw signal safety to your nervous system.

Just pause for a second.

Drop your shoulders.

Unclench your jaw.

Take a slow breath in... and out.

You don't have to hold
everything at once.

You're allowed to take this
one page at a time.

Come back to this whenever you need.

WHAT MY BODY LEARNT TO DO TO SURVIVE

Your body adapted to protect you. You might notice staying alert, scanning for danger, freezing, shutting down, people-pleasing, staying quiet, staying busy, or staying prepared.

These are not flaws.
They are learned survival responses.
You can thank them — without needing to keep living in them.

NOTICING WHAT HELPS ME SETTLE

Learning and observing what your body responds to.
What helps your body settle — even briefly?
You might notice, movement, rest, warmth, breath, music, nature, distraction, routine, writing.

Nothing here is too small to matter.
Every moment of settling is information.
The more clearly you can see what helps you, the more gently you can support yourself.
Awareness creates steadiness. Steadiness creates choice.

LET IT LAND (FREE WRITE)

This page is for whatever is sitting with you now — physically, emotionally, or mentally — after slowing down and listening to your body.

You may notice a slight shift. More clarity. More space. Or simply more awareness. You do not need to make sense of it. You do not need to stay with one feeling.

Let what you've noticed land. Let your system respond in its own way. This is how clarity settles.

WHY EXPLAINING NEVER WORKS

In every form of abuse — physical, emotional, verbal, financial, sexual, controlling — there is a pattern.

And one of the most powerful parts of that pattern is getting you to explain yourself.

This is not random.
Abuse works because it follows a method.

You were not trying to win an argument.
You were trying to be understood.

The abuser was not confused.
Their behaviour is always intentional.

This kind of abuse is repeated across relationships.
The pattern is known because it works.

In normal relationships, if someone crosses a line, you speak up. You explain why it's not okay.
And either they change — or there are consequences.
That's how healthy relationships operate.

But an abuser does not operate by healthy rules.

He knows explaining is what reasonable people do.
He relies on that.

"What do I need to do to protect myself?"

That shift is where clarity begins.

He says or does something harmful.
You react.
And suddenly you are explaining.
Clarifying.
Trying to make him see.
It feels necessary.
Like if you just say it clearly enough, calmly enough, lovingly enough,
he'll finally understand.

But this situation has been set up to work for him.

The more you explain,
the more you stay focused on fixing his behaviour
instead of seeing that the behaviour itself is the problem.
This is how control is built.

Sometimes it looks like this:

You tell him where you were.
Who you were with.
Why it took that long.
Why you answered the phone.
Why you didn't.
You explain that hitting is not okay.
That controlling you is not love.
That taking money, locking doors, shouting,
threatening — none of it is acceptable.
You say you're leaving.
He begs you not to go.
He says he understands.
He lets you talk for hours.
He agrees with you.
He apologises.
He says he loves you.

He promises change.
And for a moment, it feels like it finally landed.
You feel exhausted — but hopeful.

Then it happens again.

That is not confusion.
That is a pattern that benefits him.

Each long conversation drains you.
Each apology resets your hope.

Each "good night" makes the next bad morning harder to process.

Over time, this blurs your instincts.
The part of you that once sensed
"This isn't right"
starts to question itself.

You begin to think:
– Maybe I'm saying it wrong
– Maybe I need to try harder
– Maybe if I show him how much it hurts
– Maybe if I show him how much I love him
This is how people end up trapped and confused.

Not because they didn't fight hard enough.
But because the abuser benefits from keeping you explaining, hoping, and stuck.
The more you explain,
the more you stay inside the situation he has created.
And this is control —
even when you don't realise it's happening.

Understanding this does not mean you have to act today.
It simply shifts your focus.
Away from:
"How do I make him understand?"
And toward:
"What do I need?"

As you move forward, something important to remember:

Engagement feeds patterns.
Distance weakens them.
Noticing is everything.

CHECK-IN (USE ANYTIME)

You don't need to tick them all.
You don't need to feel "better."
Stabilisation is not linear.
Safety builds quietly.

Tick what feels true — today, not forever.

- ☐ My body feels less on edge than before
- ☐ I can notice my reactions without judging them
- ☐ I understand my nervous system better
- ☐ I feel slightly more grounded at times
- ☐ I am learning what helps me settle
- ☐ I feel more compassion toward myself
- ☐ I am allowed to move slowly
- ☐ I feel safer inside my body than I did before

Write about where you are right now — whether you feel progress, resistance, or somewhere in between.

WHAT IS BECOMING CLEARER FOR YOU?

NERVOUS SYSTEM CHECK-IN

This is a simple, proven way to bring your body out of stress and back into the present moment.

Pause here.

Take a breath.

Look around you.

Name 3 things you can see.

2 things you can feel.

1 thing you can hear.

You are here.
Right now.
Nothing else needs to be figured out in this moment.

STAGE FOUR
RECLAIMING YOUR PERCEPTION

Abuse does not only hurt the body.
It interferes with how you see yourself and the world.

Over time, you may have been told what you feel is wrong, what you remember is exaggerated,
or that what you saw
did not happen the way you think it did.

This section is about separating what is true
from what was imposed on you.

You are not here to attack yourself.
You are here to untangle what was never yours to carry.

WHEN REALITY GETS TURNED AGAINST YOU

Abusers don't say, "I am manipulating you."

Instead, they say:
– You're too sensitive.
– That never happened.
– You're remembering it wrong.
– You're crazy.
– You always overreact.
– You made me do that.

Over time, repetition becomes distortion.

If you hear something enough,
especially from someone you love or depend on,
it can begin to feel like truth.

This is how internal perception becomes unstable.

Not because you are weak —
but because you were repeatedly told your reality was incorrect.

WHEN IT ALWAYS BECOMES YOUR FAULT

He can tell you you're not doing enough — that the house isn't clean, dinner's shit, and you've "been home all day," so what have you even done? You clean more, try harder, carry more, and when you finally say you're tired, it flips. Now you're ungrateful, now you're always complaining, now you "have an attitude."

He can sleep through the night while you're up with the baby — feeding, changing, settling, running on nothing — then wake up, go to work, and tell you how exhausted he is. And when you say you're struggling, it flips. Now you're dramatic, now you "can't cope," now you're the problem.

He can look at other women, compare you to them, tell you they look better, cook better, are more put together — and still come home and eat every meal you make. And when you feel hurt, it flips. Now you're insecure, now you're crazy, now you're "starting something for no reason."

He can ignore you all day, disappear, not help, not show up — and the moment you react, it flips. Now you're the issue, now you're "too much," now everything is about how you responded, not what he did.

Nothing actually changes. The behaviour stays the same, the effort stays one-sided, the responsibility stays on you — only one thing changes: the story. And somehow, no matter what happens, it always ends with you being at fault.

WHAT ACTUALLY HAPPENED VS WHAT YOU WERE TOLD

Fact is what happened.

Narrative is the story that was wrapped around it.

For example:

Fact: He punched the wall.
Narrative: You pushed him to that point.

Fact: He took your money.
Narrative: You can't manage finances properly.

Fact: He read your messages.
Narrative: If you weren't hiding things, it wouldn't matter.

This section is about learning to separate the two.

YOU CAN STOP HERE

You can stop here if you need to.

You don't have to keep going just because you started.

Close the book.

Come back later.

Or don't.

There is no rush.

You do this in your own time.

SEPARATING FACT FROM STORY

Think of a recent or past event. Write the FACT only.
What physically happened?

Now write the NARRATIVE that was attached to it.
What were you told it meant about you?

How did that narrative make you feel about yourself?
Do not analyse yet. Just separate.

RECLAIMING YOUR PERCEPTION (REAL WORK)

This is where it gets uncomfortable. Because this part is not just about seeing him clearly — it's about seeing what you now believe about yourself because of him.

Think about what you were told repeatedly about your body, your personality, your parenting, your worth. Not once — over and over again.

What has stuck with you? How has it changed you? What do you avoid now because of it? How do you question yourself? What feels unsafe to be?

Write it:

TAKE ACTION

Not thinking your way out of it.
Testing it.
Choose one small way to go against what you were taught.
If he said your body was not perfect — wear what you avoided.
If he said you were embarrassing — speak anyway.
If he said you were "too much" — stop shrinking.

Write what you will do:

Then go and do it.
And come back to this:
What actually happened?
Did people react the way you were told they would?
Or did something else happen?

Write the truth:

NOW TAKE THIS FURTHER

This is not a one-time thing.
This is how you rebuild trust with yourself.
For the next few days, keep choosing against what you were taught.

Each time, notice what actually happens.
Not what you expect.
Not what you were told.
What is real.
Write what you notice:
What changed each time?
What stayed the same?
What are you starting to realise is not true?

NERVOUS SYSTEM CHECK-IN

This is a simple, proven way to bring your body out of stress and back into the present moment.

Pause here.

Take a breath.

Look around you.

Name 3 things you can see.

2 things you can feel.

1 thing you can hear.

You are here.
Right now.
Nothing else needs to be figured out in this moment.

The stories in this journal are illustrative examples created for educational and reflective purposes to help identify behavioural patterns and deepen understanding.

THERE IS A MOMENT WHEN YOUR PERCEPTION SHIFTS.

He says something degrading about your body.
Not as a joke.
Just casually cruel, in front of his mother.

You respond.
Not screaming.
Not crying.

You just say, "Speaking to me like this is not okay."

His mother hears you.

Instead of questioning what he said, she questions how you responded.

You're told you're disrespectful.
He's told to leave you.

Days later, he is still angry.

Not about what he said.
About how you answered.

He tells you that you're the problem.
That you've made him look bad.
That you're the one who crossed a line.

You stand there.
You listen.

And then something shifts.
The shift is quiet.
But it is enormous.

It will look different for every woman.

But when it happens, you will know.

You calmly say,
"Your mum is a smart woman. You should listen to her."

You say it evenly.
Without shouting.
Without explaining.

And you see it.

He knows.
He knows you know.

In that moment, your focus changes.

You are no longer trying to understand him.
You are no longer trying to manage him.
You are no longer trying to win.

You are looking at yourself.

You are recognising what you will and will not accept.

This is not adrenaline.
It is clarity.

And once clarity arrives, you cannot return to confusion.

This stage is dangerous.
When control shifts, reactions can escalate.

When someone senses you are no longer lost inside their narrative,
unpredictability can follow.

But this is the beginning.

Not the beginning of leaving.
Not the beginning of chaos.
The beginning of you.

The moment you stop centring him and start centring yourself.

It is tiny.
And it is enormous.

And once it happens, you cannot go back.

**Please make sure you always move in ways that keep you safe.
If you need support or safety services, please refer to the front of this journal or reach out to local services available to you.**

WHEN DID IT HAPPEN FOR YOU?

Not the worst fight.
Not the loudest moment.
The shift.
The second you stopped trying to fix him
and started seeing yourself clearly.

Write about that moment.

WHAT FOLLOWED?

Once you saw clearly, what changed?
Did you stop explaining as much?
Did you stop apologising automatically?
Did you start noticing patterns you had ignored before?

Write about the clarity that came after.

WHAT PENNY-DROP MOMENTS HAVE FOLLOWED SINCE?

The small internal realisations
that quietly changed everything.
"I can't believe I tolerated that."
"I blamed myself for that."
"Thank God I see it now."

List them.

WHAT HAVE YOU TAKEN BACK?

Your voice?
Your standards?
Your silence?
Your ability to say no?
Your ability to walk away emotionally before you physically leave?

Write it down.

A SOFT LANDING BACK TO YOURSELF

This has been heavy. Necessary — but still heavy. Pause here. Breathe. Nothing to fix. Just space for you.

What part of me deserves more space to breathe or exist freely this month?

What is one thing I can do over the next few weeks to make things feel a little lighter for me?

What do I want to feel more of and do more of this month — and how can I support myself in it?

CLARITY IS POWERFUL

But clarity does not remove risk.

People who rely on control do not respond well to losing it.
When you begin to see clearly, you must also move wisely.

This is not about provoking.
This is not about announcing your awareness.
This is about strengthening yourself quietly.

Take back what was taken.
Rebuild what was eroded.
Reclaim your standards.

And move in ways that keep you safe.

Clarity doesn't always make things easier.

It makes them real.

PAUSE BEFORE YOU CONTINUE

Take a breath before moving on.

What you've just seen is a lot.

You don't need to hold all of it at once.

Let your body settle.

Then continue when you're ready.

LEAVING DOESN'T HAPPEN ALL AT ONCE

It happens in three stages.
The first is: you leave in your mind.
There comes a point where something shifts.
You stop trying.
You stop believing it's going to change.
You might still be there.
You might still be having sex with him.
You might still be playing the role.
But internally... you've tapped out.
You know who he is.
You know nothing you say or do changes it.
Some days you feel numb.
Other days you hate him with every fibre of your being.
You're still there... but you're already gone.
The second is: you find the courage to leave.
And this is the hardest part.
Because by this point, you already know what's coming.
The calls.
The messages.
The pressure.
The love bombing.
You've probably left before.
You know how quickly it escalates.
For some, it's fear of being harassed.
For others, it's fear for their life.
But the decision is already made.
You're not confused anymore.
You just have to choose yourself... knowing what it's going to cost.
And the third is: you stop playing the game.
This is the part no one explains properly.

You're not "free" overnight.
You're not magically healed.
You just... start engaging less.
Less explaining.
Less reacting.
Less back and forth.
You see the manipulation for what it is —
the guilt, the blame, the "you're a bad mum" while he doesn't even show up.
And instead of getting pulled in...
you start stepping out.
Bit by bit.
Until one day, you're just... done.
No more arguing.
No more defending yourself.
No more trying to make him understand.
If there are kids — it becomes logistics.
Pick-up. Drop-off. That's it.
No emotion. No engagement. No game.
Because you finally see it clearly:
nothing you say changes anything.
And that's the moment it actually ends.
Not because he stopped —
but because you did.
And that's when your life starts coming back to you.

WHERE AM I RIGHT NOW — STAGE ONE, TWO, OR THREE?

After everything you've just read, pause here.
You don't need to have it all figured out.
You just need to be honest.

Stage one:
You're still in it mentally. You question yourself. You explain. You get pulled back in.

Stage two:
Something has shifted. You see it more clearly. You still get pulled in sometimes — but not the same way.

Stage three:
You've started stepping out. You engage less. You stop explaining. You see the pattern for what it is.
Where are you right now?

Write it:

THIS MATTERS MORE THAN THE STAGE

What is one small way you can protect your energy from here — not to prove a point or change them, but simply to protect yourself? It might look like saying less, explaining less, not responding straight away, walking away sooner, or keeping something for yourself. Write what that looks like for you right now:

And finally, what helps you feel safer, clearer, or more like yourself when you do this? You don't need to rush this or get it perfect — you are already moving. Write it:

THIS IS STILL PART OF IT

You might go back.

You might miss them.

You might question everything again.

You might feel pulled in ways that don't make sense.

That does not undo what you've seen.

Clarity doesn't disappear just because emotion shows up.

This is your process.

Your timing.

Your life.

No one else gets to define how this looks for you.

You are still moving forward — even if it doesn't feel like a straight line.

CHECK-IN

- ☐ I can identify when a narrative was imposed on me
- ☐ I can separate fact from story
- ☐ I can see how shame was built
- ☐ I recognise some of my responses as survival
- ☐ I am starting to trust my perception again
- ☐ I can make small decisions without panic — and trust them

You do not need to tick all of these.

Even one is movement.

Clarity builds slowly.

Trust rebuilds quietly.

YOU ARE STILL MOVING FORWARD

Leaving doesn't always look clean.

You might go back.
You might question everything.
You might miss them in ways that don't make sense.

That does not undo what you know.

It does not erase what you've seen.

And it does not mean you are back where you started.

You are still someone who sees it now.

Even in the moments where it feels
blurry — something in you knows.

And that knowing doesn't disappear.

It stays with you.
It grows with you.
It brings you back to yourself — again and again.

So if this feels messy...
if it feels slow...
if it feels like you're not doing it "right" —

You are.

You are still moving forward.

STAGE FIVE
RECLAIMING YOURSELF

This stage is about returning to yourself — not in theory, but in practice.

You have identified the pattern.
You have stabilised your body.
You have reclaimed your perception.

Now the focus shifts again.

Not toward the offender.
Not toward what happened.
Not toward what could have been.

Toward what is possible now.

Reclaiming yourself is not dramatic.
It is steady.
It is deliberate.
It is built in small choices that slowly restore your identity, your standards, and your sense of direction.

This is where your life begins to feel like it belongs to you again.

THIS PART IS DIFFERENT

You are no longer trying to understand what happened.

You are no longer trying to make sense of them.

You are no longer trying to stabilise what was shaken.

You are starting to come back to yourself.

That can feel unfamiliar at first.

Not because something is wrong — but because so much of your energy was focused on surviving.

This stage is not about doing everything perfectly.

It is about noticing where your life is already starting to shift back toward you.

Small choices.
Small moments.
Small returns to yourself.

That is how this rebuild happens.

AFTER EVERYTHING, WHAT DO YOU WANT BACK MORE THAN ANYTHING?

☐ My Peace

☐ My future

☐ My Confidence

☐ My Lightness

☐ My Joy

☐ My Energy

☐ Trust in myself

☐ My voice

☐ My body's sense of safety

☐ My independence

☐ Something else:

what have you already gained back so far?
Write about why that matters to you.

THE LIFE YOU GET BACK

Ordinary peace is powerful.
What would it feel like to:

- Wake up without fear?
- Eat what you want?
- Speak without rehearsing?
- Wear what feels good?
- See friends without managing reactions?
- Move through your day without threat?

Write about the small freedoms you are ready for.

PAUSE & NOTICE

What you just moved through
may have brought things up — memories, reactions, or feelings you haven't fully sat with before.

Pause here.
What are you feeling right now?

☐ Relief

☐ Sadness

☐ Anger

☐ Fear

☐ Strength

☐ Resistance

☐ Calm

☐ Confusion

☐ Something else:

There is no correct response.

Just notice.

TAKING CARE OF YOU

Rebuilding does not happen in one decision.
It happens in small ones.
What is one small way you can take care of yourself this week?

It might be:

- resting
- going for a walk
- saying no
- eating properly
- booking something
- deleting something
- not replying

Small actions build strength quietly.

WHEN YOU SEE THIS — YOU CAN'T UNSEE IT

You cannot teach him empathy.
You cannot control him.
You cannot fix him.
You cannot love him into integrity.

But you can control yourself.

You can decide where you stay.
You can decide what you accept.
You can decide how you respond.
You can decide when you walk.
You can decide what you build next.

The moment this becomes clear —
really clear —
you stop wasting energy trying to solve someone
who benefits from not changing.

And that energy comes back to you.

That is when things start aligning.

Not because he changed.

Because you did.

PROGRESS, NOT PERFECTION

You don't have to do this perfectly to move forward.

You don't have to get everything right.

You don't have to have it all figured out.

You just have to keep choosing yourself.

In small ways.

In real ways.

In whatever way you can today.

That is enough.

WHAT YOU GET TO CHOOSE NOW

Take a moment to answer these.

Can you choose where you stand and who you stand with?
□ Yes □ No

Can you decide what you tolerate?
□ Yes □ No

Can you remove yourself from a situation that harms you?
□ Yes □ No

Can you stop explaining yourself?
□ Yes □ No

Can you rebuild your confidence?
□ Yes □ No

Can you protect your peace?
□ Yes □ No

Can you change how you move from here?
□ Yes □ No

You can't change anyone else. But you can change yourself — the moment you decide to.

WHAT FREEDOM ACTUALLY FEELS LIKE

Freedom does not always look the way people imagine.
It does not always begin with celebration.
It often begins with quiet relief.

It might feel like making food without tension in your chest, showering without listening for footsteps, sleeping without bracing for a mood shift, spending money without interrogation, or speaking without rehearsing your words first.

Write about what freedom looks like in your ordinary, daily life.
Not the highlight reel.
The real version.

WHEN YOUR BODY STARTS TO RELAX

Living under control trains your body to stay alert.
When threat reduces, your system may not know what to do with calm.
Calm can feel unfamiliar at first.
What is it feeling like in your body to be:

- unmonitored
- unquestioned
- not criticised
- not managed
- not evaluated

Describe the physical feeling of beginning to feel safe again.

YOUR STORY OF STRENGTH

One day, this will not feel as close.

It will not be the centre of your thinking.
It will not organise your daily choices.
It will sit in your past — as part of your history, not your present.

When that day comes, what do you want to be able to say to yourself?

"I was strong."
"I remembered who I was."
"I chose myself."
"I protected my peace."
"I did what I needed to do — for me and my children."
"I stopped explaining."
"I trusted myself."

This is where your story shifts.

YOUR WORDS
YOUR POWER

Now write your version. Not what sounds right.
Not what you think you should say.
What is true for you. What you are proud of.
What you survived.
What you chose — even when it was hard.

Write the words your future self will look back on and know: You did it.

WHAT YOU CAN SEE NOW

When you are in it, most of your energy goes into managing them — keeping the peace, avoiding reactions, and trying not to make things worse. It is not about protecting yourself. It is about managing them. That is survival.

But when clarity comes, something shifts. You can see what that cost you — your peace, your stability, your sense of self, your body, your time, your safety.

This is where it changes. Not what you were protecting then, but what you choose to protect now.

What do you want to protect moving forward?
Write it here:

THIS STOPS WITH ME

You no longer have to live with:

- unpredictable moods
- strategic cruelty
- emotional interrogation
- constant defence
- bracing for escalation

List what you are no longer willing to normalise, and how it feels to free yourself from these things. How have your days changed?

A LIFE THAT FEELS LIKE MINE

Rebuilding is not only serious.
It can also be quietly exciting.
What are small things you can now explore?

- A course?
- A trip?
- A change in routine?
- Reconnecting with someone?
- Moving house?
- Redecorating?
- Starting again in a way that feels yours?

Write about something that feels even slightly hopeful.

WHAT YOU GET TO CHOOSE NOW

Set aside the version of you that was adapting to survive.

What goals feel possible now?

They can be small.
They can be big.
They can be quiet or completely life-changing.

You get to choose.

Write three goals that belong to you — not to anyone else's expectations.

RECLAIMING DESIRE

For a long time, your focus may have been on keeping things calm, avoiding reactions, or managing someone else. Your wants didn't disappear — they just got quieter.

Now, notice what is starting to come back.

☐ I'm noticing things I want

☐ I'm thinking about what would feel good for me

☐ I'm allowing myself to imagine a different kind of life

☐ I'm feeling drawn to things that feel like me

☐ I'm wanting peace, space, or quiet without guilt

☐ I'm catching myself thinking about what I would choose

Now pause and notice:
What are you starting to want again?
What feels like it belongs to you?
Write it here.

RECLAIMING SELF-TRUST

Self-trust rebuilds through action. Not big, perfect moments. It's small choices where you begin to rely on yourself again.

Notice what is already shifting.

☐ I'm making decisions without over-explaining them

☐ I'm trusting my instinct instead of second-guessing

☐ I'm following through on what I choose

☐ I'm leaving things that aren't mine to carry

☐ I'm choosing myself, even when it feels uncomfortable

☐ I know what feels right without needing reassurance

Now pause and notice:
What are you starting to trust about yourself again?
What feels like it doesn't belong to you anymore?
Write it here.

RECLAIMING PACE

You don't need to change everything at once. This is about small, steady shifts that begin to make your life feel different.

Notice how you are starting to move through your days.

□ I'm slowing down instead of reacting straight away

□ I'm taking a moment before responding

□ I'm doing small things that support me

□ I'm allowing myself to rest without guilt

□ I'm creating moments of calm in my day

□ I'm choosing what feels better, not just what feels familiar

Now pause and notice:
What feels different in your day?
What feels slightly easier or calmer?
Write it here.

RECLAIMING STANDARDS

Standards are about what you no longer accept — and what you choose to protect moving forward.

Notice what is becoming clear for you now.

□ I'm recognising behaviour I will no longer tolerate

□ I'm feeling clear "no" responses to things I used to allow

□ I'm no longer explaining away what hurts me

□ I'm noticing when something doesn't feel right

□ I'm becoming clear on what I will and won't accept

□ I'm feeling more certain about what I deserve

Now pause and notice:
What are you no longer willing to accept?
What feels non-negotiable now?
Write it here.

A QUIET SHIFT

Take a moment to notice where you are now.

□ I feel clearer than I did before

□ I feel stronger in ways I didn't expect

□ I can see things for what they are

□ I am less focused on changing someone else

□ I am more focused on myself and my life

□ I trust what I feel more than I used to

□ I feel moments of calm or relief

□ I can imagine something different for myself

Tick what feels true.

You don't need to force this.
You don't need to have it all figured out.

But something has shifted.

And you can feel it.

You are not who you were when you started this.

You see things differently now.

And you don't have to ignore that anymore.

STAGE SIX
LIVING WITH CLARITY

You are not the same woman who opened this journal.

You see more now.
You recognise more.
You trust yourself more.

Your life is no longer organised around confusion.
It is no longer organised around fear.
It is no longer organised around managing someone else's behaviour.

It is organised around you.

This stage is not about processing what happened.
It is about living differently because of what you now understand.

This is integration.
This is steadiness.
This is clarity.

WHEN LIFE FEELS CALM AGAIN

Nothing big happened.
I made coffee.
The kids were loud.
The house was messy.

My phone went off.
And for a second, I noticed something.

There was no drop in my stomach.
No rush of panic.
No thought of what I needed to say or fix.

I didn't feel like I was about to get in trouble.
I didn't feel like I had to manage anything.
I just kept making my coffee.

And it hit me — quietly, but clearly.

My life is not built around someone else's reactions anymore.
There is nothing to brace for.
There is nothing to decode.
There is nothing waiting to flip.

It's just... my life.

That might sound small.

But it's not.

That is what calm feels like when it's real.

IF THIS FEELS LIKE TOO MUCH

If this ever feels like too much...

come back to this:

You are not behind.

You are not doing this wrong.

You are not starting over.

You are moving through something real.

And you are still here.

That matters more than anything.

CHECKING IN WITH YOURSELF

Pause for a moment.
How are you feeling lately — not in your past, not in the relationship —
but in your actual life now?
Do you feel calmer?
More steady?
More clear?

Do you still get moments where things feel heavy?
Do you notice how different your reactions are now?

Just notice. Not to judge. Not to fix.
Just to see yourself clearly.

WHAT HAS CHANGED

Something is different.

□ I feel calmer in my body

□ I am not constantly bracing

□ I don't analyse everything the same way

□ I don't feel responsible for someone else's behaviour

□ I trust what I feel

□ I notice things earlier

□ I speak up when something doesn't feel right

□ I say things I wouldn't have said before

□ I set boundaries I used to avoid

□ I leave situations sooner

□ I don't engage in things that drain me

□ I feel more like myself

Something has shifted.

SEEING IT WHILE IT'S HAPPENING

You might still get triggered sometimes.
A tone.
A message.
A memory.
Before — that would have taken over your whole body.
Your chest tight.
Your heart racing.
Adrenaline pumping through you.
Your mind going straight to worst-case scenarios.
Overthinking.
Replaying.
Trying to figure it out.
Trying to fix it.
Trying to get ahead of what might happen next.
It felt like you had to.
But now...
You still notice it.
But instead of it taking over — there's a gap.
Your body still remembers.
But it's learning.
It's calmer.
That's awareness.
It doesn't mean you don't feel it.
It means you can see it while you're feeling it.
And sometimes — that's enough to stop it from pulling you all the way under.
Not every time.
Not perfectly.
But differently.
And that difference?
That's the work you've done.

Because when you didn't understand what was happening — when you were caught in it — that's where the control had power.

Confusion benefits them.

Not knowing benefits them.

But you see it now.
And once you see it — you can't unsee it.

That is your power.

WHAT HAVE YOU STARTED TO RECOGNISE THAT YOU DIDN'T UNDERSTAND BEFORE?

THAT DOESN'T WORK ON ME ANYMORE

There may still be moments where you see him.
For children.
For legal reasons.
By chance.
That does not undo your progress.
You are not the same woman in those moments.
You are clearer.
You are steadier.
You are not there to manage him anymore.
You are there for your children.
And for yourself.
And this matters — because the behaviour may not stop.
The messages.
The accusations.
The lies.
The attempts to pull you back in.
Saying things to get a reaction.
Twisting things to make you defend yourself.
Making you look like the problem.
Trying to provoke, confuse, or pull you into explaining yourself again.
That is the pattern.
And this is where it changes.
You see it now.
So instead of getting pulled into it — you notice it.
And you choose differently.
You choose what you respond to.
You choose what you ignore.
You choose what you walk away from.
And what you no longer participate in at all.
This is power.

WHAT GAMES, CONVERSATIONS, OR BEHAVIOURS HAVE YOU STOPPED PARTICIPATING IN?
WHAT DO YOU CHOOSE INSTEAD NOW?

Everything Has Shifted

Your life is not organised around fear anymore.

It is not organised around someone else's moods.

It is organised around you.

Your time.
Your energy.
Your peace.
Your children.
Your future.

That is not small.

That is everything.

THIS IS THE VERSION OF YOU THAT CAME THROUGH THIS.

Not who you were before.
Not who you were made to be.

Who you choose to be now.

I am someone who ____________________________________

I trust myself to ______________________________________

I no longer accept ____________________________________

I choose ____

I care for myself by ___________________________________

I support myself by ____________________________________

I show up for myself by ________________________________

This is who I am now — and I stand by her.

You don't have to have everything figured out.

You don't have to rebuild your entire life overnight.

You just have to keep choosing yourself.

Again.
And again.
And again.

That is enough.

THIS WAS NOT SMALL

You do not have to be grateful for what happened.
It should not have happened.
But you can recognise what you did with it.
You faced it.
You saw it.
You got out.
You changed.
That is not small.
What are you proud of in yourself?

WHERE IT SHIFTED

There was a point where things changed.
You saw it clearly.
You stopped explaining it away.
You stopped minimising it.
You stopped trying to make it make sense.
And you made a decision.
That moment matters.
Because that is where this shifted.
Not everything. But enough.
Enough to choose differently.
Enough to move.
Enough to get out.
That is your breakthrough.

READ THIS SLOWLY

I need you to understand something.

What you just did is not normal.

You walked yourself out of something that breaks people.

You saw what was happening.
You faced it.
You untangled it.
And you chose differently.

That is not small.

That is not luck.

That is you.

And whether anyone else sees it or not —
I do.

I am proud of you.

In a real, grounded, human way.

Because I know what it takes to do what you just did.

And you did it.

SEEING IT ALL FOR WHAT IT WAS

Sometimes you might catch yourself wishing things were different.
Wishing it could have worked.

But you know now.

You know who he is. You see the patterns.
You see the games.
And in a strange way — that takes the pressure off.
Because you're not trying to figure it out anymore.
You're not trying to fix it. You see it clearly.

That awareness didn't stop with him.
You see yourself more clearly now too.
Where you stayed.
Where you ignored things.
Where you needed more care — from others,
and from yourself.

You can't unsee any of this now. And that's not a bad thing.
It's the most important thing.
Because from here — you get to choose yourself differently.

You get to love yourself harder.
You get to be fiercer.
More protective.
More honest about what you need.
You get to stop settling.
Stop shrinking.
Stop explaining yourself away.
You get to choose the life you actually want.
Because you are worthy of all of it.

WRITE ABOUT WHAT'S COMING UP FOR YOU

THE ONLY DIRECTION FROM HERE — IS UP

This is your life.
You get to choose what it looks like from here.
There are no rules. No limits. No one else to shape it for you.

Just you.

So take a moment and think about it.

You don't have to make it make sense. You don't have to have it all figured out.
Just start seeing it.
Write down what your "up" looks like.
Big or small. Simple or bold.
This is your life now.
And you get to choose all of it.

What kind of life do you actually want to wake up to every day?

Where do you want to go, see, or experience?

DREAM BIGGER THAN YOU EVER HAVE — JUST BECAUSE YOU CAN

What would success look like for you (not anyone else)?

What excites you right now, even a little bit?

What do you want — just because you want it?

What are you no longer available for?

FINDING YOU AGAIN

If you're here,
you made it to the end of this.
That matters.
Even if it didn't feel clear.
Even if it felt messy.
Even if you had to stop and start,
or skip parts,
or come back more than once.
You still showed up.
And that's not something small.
There was nothing you needed to do perfectly here.
There was nothing you needed to "get right."
This was never about doing it properly.
It was about being honest,
in whatever way you could manage.
You don't have to leave this behind now.
You can come back to it—
as many times as you need to.
Not because you're going backwards,
but because this is what it looks like
to keep choosing yourself.
And choosing yourself again and again
is how you care for yourself,
how you begin to soften,
how you slowly come back to who you are.
It's enough to keep you moving forward.
It's enough to keep you growing.
It's enough to keep you healing.
So keep choosing you.

Made in United States
Cleveland, OH
06 November 2026

47653965R00080